LEVEL C
Book 2

MULTIPLE SKILLS
SERIES: Reading

Third Edition

Richard A. Boning

SRA McGraw-Hill

Columbus, Ohio

A Division of The McGraw·Hill Companies

SRA/McGraw-Hill

A Division of The **McGraw·Hill** *Companies*

Send all inquiries to:
SRA/McGraw-Hill
250 Old Wilson Bridge Road
Suite 310
Worthington, Ohio 43085

ISBN 0-02-688419-4

3 4 5 6 7 8 9 SCG 02 01 00 99 98

PURPOSE

The *Multiple Skills Series* is a nonconsumable reading program designed to develop a cluster of key reading skills and to integrate these skills with each other and with the other language arts. *Multiple Skills* is also diagnostic, making it possible for you to identify specific types of reading skills that might be causing difficulty for individual students.

FOR WHOM

The twelve levels of the *Multiple Skills Series* are geared to students who comprehend on the pre-first- through ninth-grade reading levels.

- The Picture Level is for children who have not acquired a basic sight vocabulary.
- The Preparatory 1 Level is for children who have developed a limited basic sight vocabulary.
- The Preparatory 2 Level is for children who have a basic sight vocabulary but are not yet reading on the first-grade level.
- Books A through I are appropriate for students who can read on grade levels one through nine respectively. Because of their high interest level, the books may also be used effectively with students functioning at these levels of competence in other grades.

The **Multiple Skills Series Placement Tests** will help you determine the appropriate level for each student.

PLACEMENT TESTS

The Elementary Placement Test (for grades Pre-1 through 3) and the Midway Placement Tests (for grades 4–9) will help you place each student properly. The tests consist of representative units selected from the series. The test books contain two forms, X and Y. One form may be used for placement and the second as a posttest to measure progress. The tests are easy to administer and score. Blackline Masters are provided for worksheets and student performance profiles.

THE BOOKS

This third edition of the *Multiple Skills Series* maintains the quality and focus that have distinguished this program for over 25 years. The series includes four books at each level, Picture Level through Level I. Each book in the Picture Level through Level B contains 25 units. Each book in Level C through Level I contains 50 units. The units within each book increase in difficulty. The books within a level also increase in difficulty—Level A, Book 2 is slightly more difficult than Level A, Book 1, and so on. This gradual increase in difficulty permits students to advance from one book to the next and from one level to the next without frustration.

Each book contains an **About This Book** page, which explains the skills to the students and shows them how to approach reading the selections and questions. In the lowest levels, you should read About This Book to the children.

The questions that follow each unit are designed to develop specific reading skills. In the lowest levels, you should read the questions to the children. In Level C, the question pattern in each unit is

1. Title (main idea)
2. Stated detail
3. Stated detail
4. Inference or conclusion
5. Vocabulary

The **Language Activity Pages** (LAP) in each level consist of four parts: Exercising Your Skill, Expanding Your Skill, Exploring Language, and Expressing Yourself. These pages lead the students beyond the book through a broadening spiral of writing, speaking, and other individual and group language activities that apply, extend, and integrate the skills being developed. You may use all, some, or none of the activities in any LAP; however, some LAP activities depend on preceding ones. In the lowest levels, you should read the LAPs to the children.

In Levels C–I, each set of Language Activity Pages focuses on a particular skill developed through the book. Emphasis progresses from the most concrete to the most abstract:

First LAP	Details
Second LAP	Vocabulary
Third LAP	Main ideas
Last LAP	Inferences and conclusions

SESSIONS

The *Multiple Skills Series* is an individualized reading program that may be used with small groups or an entire class. Short sessions are the most effective. Use a short session every day or every other day, completing a few units in each session. Time allocated to the Language Activity Pages depends on the abilities of the individual students.

SCORING

Students should record their answers on the reproducible worksheets. The worksheets make scoring easier and provide uniform records of the children's work. Using worksheets also avoids consuming the books.

Because it is important for the students to know how they are progressing, you should score the units as soon as they've been completed. Then you can discuss the questions and activities with the students and encourage them to justify their responses. Many of the LAPs are open-ended and do not lend themselves to an objective score; for this reason, there are no answer keys for these pages.

About This Book

A careful reader thinks about the writer's words and pays attention to what the story or article is mainly about. A careful reader also "reads between the lines" because a writer does not tell the reader everything. A careful reader tries to figure out the meaning of new words too. As you read the stories and articles in this book, you will practice all of these reading skills.

First you will read a story and choose a good title for it. The title will tell something about the **main idea** of the article or story. To choose a good title, you must know what the story or article is mainly about.

The next two questions will ask you about facts that are stated in the story or article. To answer these questions, read carefully. Pay attention to the **details.**

The fourth question will ask you to figure out **something the writer doesn't tell you directly.** For example, you might read that Dr. Fujihara received an emergency call, drove to Elm Street, and rushed into a house. Even though the writer doesn't tell you directly, you can figure out that Dr. Fujihara knows how to drive and that someone in the house is probably sick. You use the information the author provides plus your own knowledge and experience to figure out what is probably true.

The last question will ask you to tell the meaning of a word in the story or article. You can figure out what the word means by studying its **context**—the other words and sentences in the story. Read the following sentences.

> Ted pulled and pulled on the line. The big fish pulled too. After more than an hour, Ted was finally able to pull the fish out of the water. He had caught his first *salmon.*

Did you figure out that a salmon is a kind of fish? What clues in the story helped you figure this out?

This book will help you practice your reading skills. As you learn to use all of these skills together, you will become a better reader.

Martha Washington was the wife of George Washington, the first President of the United States. As a child, Martha probably had no idea that her life would become so exciting.

Growing up, Martha lived on a large farm in the South. She and her sisters and brothers liked to go fishing or to run races with each other.

There were not many schools then, so Martha learned at home how to read, write, spell, sew, and cook. She often shared her favorite *dishes* with her pet squirrel, Maybelle.

All that she learned as a child helped Martha later when she became First Lady of the United States.

---

1. The best title is—
   (A) Martha Washington as a Child
   (B) Why Squirrels Are Good Pets
   (C) Fun on Southern Farms
   (D) How to Go to School at Home

2. Martha Washington grew up—
   (A) in the city   (B) in an apartment
   (C) in the West   (D) on a farm

3. Martha learned school subjects—
   (A) in a schoolhouse   (B) at home
   (C) in another town   (D) in the summer

4. As a child, Martha was probably—
   (A) sad   (B) lonely
   (C) happy   (D) angry

5. The word "dishes" in line nine means—
   (A) kinds of work   (B) kinds of food
   (C) ideas   (D) plates

Jason Hardman was ten years old when his family moved. Jason liked the new town, except for one thing—it had no library. So Jason decided to start a library. First he talked to the mayor and the town council. They said they "would think about it." That was not what Jason had hoped to hear, but it did not stop him. Finally, they gave in. With help from some grown-ups, Jason started a library in the town hall cellar. The library grew, and so did Jason's fame. There were newspaper stories about him, and he appeared on TV. Then he got an award from the President of the United States. Jason Hardman was named "America's Youngest Librarian," a title he richly *deserved*.

1. The best title is—
   (A) Getting My Way
   (B) Libraries
   (C) Reading Books Is Important
   (D) America's Youngest Librarian

2. Jason's new town had—
   (A) no library
   (B) no friends
   (C) no stores
   (D) no schools

3. Jason got an award from—
   (A) a newspaper
   (B) a TV station
   (C) the President
   (D) the mayor

4. You can tell that Jason liked—
   (A) the mayor
   (B) going to school
   (C) the town council
   (D) to read

5. The word "deserved" in line ten means—
   (A) missed
   (B) earned
   (C) lost
   (D) hated

Mrs. Davis was very sad. She had been sick and now she couldn't hear anymore. She was sad because she had a baby to take care of. When the baby cried, Mrs. Davis couldn't hear him.

Then Mrs. Davis got Banjo. Banjo was a dog trained to help people who can't hear. When the baby cried, Banjo ran to Mrs. Davis and *reared* up on its hind legs. Banjo also "told" Mrs. Davis when the telephone was ringing or when someone was knocking at the door.

Mrs. Davis was happy because she had Banjo to help her.

---

1. The best title is—
   (A) Looking for a Lost Dog
   (B) Mrs. Davis Went to the Doctor
   (C) How Banjo Helped Mrs. Davis
   (D) Taking Care of a Pet Dog

2. The story says that Mrs. Davis—
   (A) could not see   (B) could not hear
   (C) disliked dogs   (D) loved cats

3. Banjo "told" Mrs. Davis when—
   (A) her food was cooked   (B) her car needed gas
   (C) the TV was on   (D) the telephone rang

4. Mrs. Davis probably—
   (A) loved Banjo   (B) disliked Banjo
   (C) did not own Banjo   (D) had no children

5. The word "reared" in line six means—
   (A) slept   (B) stood
   (C) fell   (D) swam

One of the world's greatest runners was told he would never walk again. Glenn Cunningham grew up on a Kansas farm. Each morning he and his brother Floyd would run one mile to school. Their job was to light the stove that heated the room. One day the stove *exploded*, killing Floyd. Glenn's legs were burned badly. Doctors thought he would never walk again, but his mother made him try. It took four long, painful years, but Glenn did walk again. Soon after, he began to run. Before he was done, Glenn became the world's best in the one-mile run. Today Glenn Cunningham, the man who wouldn't take "you'll never walk" for an answer, is a model for those who believe in themselves.

---

1. The best title is—
   (A) Growing Up
   (B) Running for Fun
   (C) A Bad Stove
   (D) Then I'll Run!

2. Glenn Cunningham grew up in—
   (A) New York   (B) a hospital
   (C) Kansas   (D) Nebraska

3. Glenn was hurt—
   (A) at school   (B) on the road
   (C) at home   (D) in the barn

4. Glenn's mother—
   (A) was angry   (B) did not like Floyd
   (C) hated the school (D) helped him walk

5. The word "exploded" in line four means—
   (A) got cold   (B) blew up
   (C) broke   (D) disappeared

Mother's Day is an important day. It's a day when children can show their mothers how much they love them. Many children give flowers to their mothers. This makes them very happy.

Most of the people who live near Mrs. Taylor's flower store are poor. The children don't have any money to buy flowers. Mrs. Taylor helps them. The children work one hour for Mrs. Taylor. They clean the windows, sweep the sidewalk, and *mop* the floor in the store. Then Mrs. Taylor gives each of them flowers to take home for their mothers. The mothers who live near Mrs. Taylor's store all have a wonderful Mother's Day.

---

1. The best title is—
   (A) Flowers for Mother's Day
   (B) A Mean Woman
   (C) Mrs. Taylor's Birthday
   (D) Lazy Children

2. Most people who live near Mrs. Taylor's store are—
   (A) all tall
   (B) rich
   (C) poor
   (D) never home

3. When the children work for Mrs. Taylor, they—
   (A) drive a truck
   (B) grow flowers
   (C) sweep the sidewalk
   (D) paint the store

4. You can tell that Mrs. Taylor is—
   (A) a teacher
   (B) unhappy
   (C) not liked
   (D) a kind woman

5. The word "mop" in line seven means—
   (A) break
   (B) wash
   (C) sell
   (D) hurt

Elephants use their trunks the way people use their hands. At the end of the trunk are parts that act like fingers. These allow elephants to do wonderful things. They pick up their food—parts of trees or maybe just a peanut. They use their trunks to drink water or to *spray* the water over their bodies to cool off. Because elephants do not see well, they use their trunks as "eyes." They do not walk where their trunks cannot feel the ground.

Carole, a twenty-two-year-old elephant at the San Diego Wild Animal Park, paints with her trunk. At her trainer's order, Carole swings a brush across a canvas. Her paintings are sold to make money for the park.

---

1. The best title is—
   (A) Elephants' Trunks
   (B) An Elephant Named Carole
   (C) How Elephants Find Food
   (D) The Elephant

2. Elephants pick up objects with their—
   (A) feet
   (B) fingers
   (C) teeth
   (D) trunks

3. Elephants do not—
   (A) eat tree parts
   (B) see well
   (C) eat peanuts
   (D) like water

4. In the dark an elephant can find its way with its—
   (A) eyes
   (B) ears
   (C) trunk
   (D) tail

5. The word "spray" in line four means—
   (A) shoot out in drops
   (B) put soap into
   (C) step into
   (D) warm up

Her name is Florence Griffith Joyner, but most people call her Flo Jo. She is one of the greatest athletes in the world. During the 1988 Olympic Games, Flo Jo won four medals—three gold and one silver—in running. Since then, she has become famous for her running and for the running clothes she makes.

All this *fame* did not come easily to Flo Jo. For four years, she held two jobs and trained in her spare time. She ran and ran, then ran some more. Often she did not sleep for two whole days. "Why," Flo Jo was asked, "did you work so hard?" Her simple answer was, "I wanted to be the best."

1. The best title is—
   (A) The Olympic Games
   (B) How to Make Your Own Clothes
   (C) A Great Athlete
   (D) Flo Jo as a Child

2. In the 1988 Olympic Games, Flo Jo won—
   (A) one medal　　　　　　(B) two medals
   (C) three medals　　　　　(D) four medals

3. While training for the Olympics, Flo Jo had to—
   (A) work two jobs　　　　(B) sleep a lot
   (C) swim each day　　　　(D) cook her own meals

4. To win in the Olympic Games, a person must—
   (A) sleep for two days　　(B) never eat
   (C) make clothes　　　　　(D) train very hard

5. The word "fame" in line six means—
   (A) being tall　　　　　　(B) being sleepy
   (C) being well-known　　　(D) being in space

You can find kids working at many kinds of jobs. But not too many have the job Kurt Sanders has. He does stunts on TV and in the movies. Kurt was only seven years old when he did his first stunt. He had to run in front of a speeding car! Another time he was asked to fall off a high ladder. One time he was put into a burning house. Kurt had to wait until the floor burned through. Then he fell into the room below.

Of course these stunts are *risky*. But Kurt has never been hurt. He does each one just the way he is told. Kurt's not sure, though, how long he will go on doing stunts. It's not that he's scared. "Maybe I'll become a baseball player," he says.

1. The best title is—
   (A) Jobs for Kids
   (B) Stunt Kid
   (C) TV
   (D) Movies

2. In Kurt's first stunt, he worked with a —
   (A) ladder   (B) burning house
   (C) flight of stairs (D) speeding car

3. Kurt says he—
   (A) was burned in a stunt   (B) cannot be hurt
   (C) may play ball   (D) will never quit stunts

4. Kurt—
   (A) will be hurt soon   (B) fears doing stunts
   (C) is careful in stunts (D) doesn't like to obey

5. The word "risky" in line eight means—
   (A) easy   (B) dangerous
   (C) hard   (D) boring

Mrs. Neumann *admired* cats so much that she had thirty-eight of them as pets. One day she decided to have a swimming pool built in her backyard. When the workers came to build the pool, Mrs. Neumann said, "I want the swimming pool to be in the shape of a mouse." She thought that with so many pet cats she should have at least one mouse.

The workers thought it was a funny idea. They built a pool that looked like a mouse. It even had a tail and whiskers. The cats, however, did not seem to notice the shape of the pool. They only used it for drinking.

---

1. The best title is—
   (A) A Pet Dog
   (B) A Hospital for Cats
   (C) A Pool Shaped Like a Mouse
   (D) Going for a Swim

2. Mrs. Neumann had—
   (A) 12 dogs   (B) 32 fish
   (C) 38 cats   (D) 15 mice

3. The swimming pool was built to look like a—
   (A) cat   (B) box
   (C) flower   (D) mouse

4. Mrs. Neumann's cats used the swimming pool when they were—
   (A) hungry   (B) thirsty
   (C) dirty   (D) sleepy

5. The word "admired" in line one means—
   (A) washed   (B) liked
   (C) lost   (D) hated

Children have enjoyed eating jellybeans for many years. David Klein thought that grown-ups would eat more of them too, if there were jellybeans with unusual flavors. So David, who calls himself "Mr. Jelly Belly," made some jellybeans with *peculiar* flavors.

David calls his jellybeans "Jelly Bellies." He makes nearly forty different flavors. Some of them are watermelon, coconut, baked apple, and root beer. He even has coffee and buttered popcorn Jelly Bellies.

For some holidays, new flavors are brought out. A few times at Thanksgiving, people were able to buy pumpkin Jelly Bellies. What new flavors would you suggest?

---

1. The best title is—
   (A) A Box of Candy
   (B) Baked Apples
   (C) Jelly Bellies
   (D) Delicious Candy Bars

2. David Klein calls himself—
   (A) Mr. Root Beer   (B) Mr. Flavor
   (C) Mr. Pumpkin   (D) Mr. Jelly Belly

3. New Jelly Belly flavors are brought out for some—
   (A) seasons   (B) holidays
   (C) movies   (D) sports

4. People like food made from pumpkins around—
   (A) Flag Day   (B) Thanksgiving
   (C) Labor Day   (D) Valentine's Day

5. The word "peculiar" in line four means—
   (A) unusual   (B) unhappy
   (C) soap   (D) lazy

Olna Daves' friends like her stories. Her favorite one is about a truck driver who could not read. Every day he would find some youngster to read to him the list of places he had to go. He thought grown-ups would laugh at him. Then one day the truck driver met Olna. She did not laugh at him. Instead, she taught him how to read. Olna learned that many grown-ups in her county could not read. She decided to start a school just for them.

That was more than twenty years ago, but Olna is still *tutoring* adults in how to read. To help pay for her school, Olna takes sewing jobs. "I don't mind spending my money," she says. "It's so nice to see somebody learn to read."

---

1. The best title is—
   - (A) Truck Drivers
   - (B) Reading Teacher
   - (C) How to Read
   - (D) Sewing to Teach

2. Olna's first student was a—
   - (A) friend
   - (B) young boy
   - (C) truck driver
   - (D) police officer

3. In order to help pay for her school, Olna—
   - (A) sells fruit
   - (B) takes sewing jobs
   - (C) charges students
   - (D) sells stories

4. The best word to describe Olna is—
   - (A) strong
   - (B) funny
   - (C) caring
   - (D) lazy

5. The word "tutoring" in line eight means—
   - (A) reading
   - (B) teaching
   - (C) sewing
   - (D) finding

Coral reefs are beautiful gardens under the sea. The corals may look like branching trees, large domes, or flower blossoms. Many sea animals live among the coral. They paint the gardens bright shades of orange, yellow, and purple.

Coral reefs are made of the skeletons of tiny sea animals called polyps. A polyp's skeleton grows outside its body. When the polyp dies, the skeleton is left. Coral reefs are formed of *billions* and billions of these tiny skeletons.

Coral reefs are found mostly in warm, shallow waters. The Great Barrier Reef of Australia is the largest coral reef in the world. It is about 1,250 miles long.

1. The best title is—
   (A) Bright Shades
   (B) The Great Barrier Reef
   (C) How Polyps Form Skeletons
   (D) Gardens Under the Sea

2. Coral reefs are made of—
   (A) plants
   (B) colorful fish
   (C) animal skeletons
   (D) branching trees

3. A skeleton of a polyp grows—
   (A) upside down
   (B) outside its body
   (C) from stone
   (D) inside its body

4. The story suggests that Australia's Great Barrier Reef is found in—
   (A) warm, shallow water
   (B) a city
   (C) cold, deep water
   (D) a long river

5. The word "billions" in line seven means—
   (A) about 100
   (B) hardly any
   (C) a few
   (D) many millions

A. Exercising Your Skill

Do you own a pet? List your favorite pets on your paper.

1. _____ 2. _____
3. _____ 4. _____

Most people keep pets because they are like friends. Some animals are more than friends. These animals have been taught to do very special things. Read the story below.

You may have heard about dogs that are trained to help blind people find their way around. But do you know about dogs who help people who cannot hear? About two million people in this country are deaf. They cannot hear any sounds. Another eleven million people have some kind of hearing problem. Imagine not being able to hear the sound of an alarm clock, or a car horn, or a telephone. That is what hearing-ear dogs do. They act as their master's ears. Almost any kind of dog can be trained to be a hearing-ear dog. The dog must be young, so it will be able to work for many years. It takes about four months to train a hearing-ear dog. The first two months are spent teaching the dog simple things, like *come here*, *sit*, and *heel*. After that, the dog is ready to learn the sounds its master needs to know.

On your own paper, write four facts you learned from reading the paragraph above.

B. Expanding Your Skill

Read the story below. On your own paper, write the number of the blank and a word that best fills the blank.

When people ask for a hearing-ear (1)_____, they must name the three (2)_____ they want the dog to "hear" for them. Most people list a beeping (3)_____, a ringing (4)_____, and the sound of someone knocking at the (5)_____ . Of course, deaf parents want their dog to warn them of a crying (6)_____ .

C. Exploring Language

Many different animals make good pets. Different people like animals for different reasons. The facts about an animal can help you know why someone likes it for a pet.

Think about the pet you already own, or choose a favorite pet from the list you made in Part A. Plan and write a paragraph about your favorite pet. On your own paper, answer these questions:

1. What four facts do I know about this animal?

   _____   _____

   _____   _____

2. Why does this animal make a good pet?_____

3. Would other people like this pet? Why?_____

Use your answers to help you write a paragraph that begins like the one below. When the paragraph is complete, write a title that tells something special about the pet.

> _____(Title)_____
>
> A *(name the pet)* is my favorite pet because _____
> _____
> _____
> _____

D. Expressing Yourself

Choose one of these things.

1. Prepare a talk about your pet. Try to include pictures if you have them. Give the talk to your classmates.

2. Draw a picture of yourself and your pet doing what you like best. If you do not have a pet, choose one you would like to own. Then draw your picture.

3. Write a story in which the hero is a pet. You may have the story tell about the pet saving someone's life.

Many people are afraid to fly. They always drive, or take a bus or train. When they have to travel far, the trips take a long time. Airplanes would be much faster.

Dr. Siegal teaches people about how not to be afraid of flying. They learn that airplanes are really safe. They also learn how to stay calm when flying. Dr. Siegal sometimes takes people for a ride in his airplane.

Most of the people who have gone to Dr. Siegal now love to fly. They say that Dr. Siegal has *erased* their fear of flying.

---

1. The best title is—
   (A) A Long Bus Ride
   (B) Learning How to Build an Airplane
   (C) Helping People Who Are Afraid to Fly
   (D) A Close Race

2. Dr. Siegal teaches that airplanes are—
   (A) slow   (B) safe
   (C) dangerous   (D) little

3. Some people go with Dr. Siegal for—
   (A) a bus ride   (B) a fine dinner
   (C) a train ride   (D) a plane ride

4. From the story you can tell that airplanes—
   (A) are very slow   (B) are not dangerous
   (C) are always small   (D) have TV sets

5. The word "erased" in line nine means—
   (A) gotten rid of   (B) placed
   (C) painted   (D) read

You've probably seen blimps flying above football games. The TV cameras on board these pickle-shaped balloons give us wonderful pictures of the games, and the flashing lights tell us what tires to buy. Have you ever wondered how this kind of airship got its name?

There are several kinds of airships. Some are balloons inside frames and some are balloons without frames. A blimp is called a *nonrigid* airship because the bag that holds the gas doesn't have a frame. The gas in the bag is what gives this airship its shape—and what lifts it into the sky. Without gas in the bag, the bag is limp. The U.S. Navy called these airships Class B nonrigid airships. People soon called them B-limps or blimps.

---

1. The best title is—
   (A) B-Limps
   (B) Watching a Football Game
   (C) Blimps and Airplanes
   (D) Bags in Flight

2. A blimp gets its shape from—
   (A) its pilot   (B) air
   (C) gas   (D) steel

3. Blimps are shaped like—
   (A) airplanes   (B) basketballs
   (C) pickles   (D) boxes

4. The story suggests that blimps are—
   (A) easy to fly   (B) out of date
   (C) never seen   (D) used for advertising

5. The word "nonrigid" in line six means—
   (A) winged   (B) stiff
   (C) plastic   (D) limp

Many American soldiers lost their lives during the Revolutionary War. Hundreds of others were wounded. One of these was Margaret Cochran Corbin.

When Margaret's husband, John Corbin, joined the army, she went with him. Like many other soldiers' wives, Margaret washed, cooked, and did other jobs for the *troops*. When John Corbin was killed in the Battle of Fort Washington, Margaret took his place behind a cannon. She fought until she was badly wounded.

When the war was over, Margaret was honored by the United States government for her bravery.

1. The best title is—
   (A) Soldiers' Wives
   (B) The Revolutionary War
   (C) Women as Soldiers
   (D) Margaret Corbin, an American Hero

2. Margaret took her husband's place—
   (A) cooking   (B) behind a cannon
   (C) at home   (D) washing dishes

3. Margaret's husband was killed at—
   (A) Mount Washington   (B) Washington, D.C.
   (C) Fort Washington   (D) Revolution Hill

4. The story suggests that most soldiers were—
   (A) women   (B) killed
   (C) men   (D) wounded

5. The word "troops" in line six means—
   (A) children   (B) town
   (C) general   (D) soldiers

Fannie Lou Hamer began life in 1917 as the 20th child of Jim and Ella Townsend. During the next 60 years, she fought for the civil rights of all people.

In 1962 many African Americans were afraid to vote, but Fannie Lou Hamer knew that voting was her right. She convinced others that they should vote too. This upset many white people. Fannie Lou was shot at, sent to jail, and beaten because of her work for civil rights.

However, this did not stop her. When she got out of jail, Fannie Lou was very angry. She went to Washington, D.C., to talk about *injustices* to black people and poor people. Other people listened and offered to help. Over the next 15 years, Fannie Lou worked hard to change the way black people and poor people were treated.

---

1. The best title is—
   (A) Voting Rights
   (B) Farm Life
   (C) Fannie Lou Hamer, Civil Rights Worker
   (D) Fannie Lou Hamer Goes to Jail

2. Fannie Lou went to jail for telling black people to—
   (A) vote   (B) eat
   (C) work   (D) go to school

3. Fannie Lou began fighting for the right to vote in—
   (A) 1917   (B) 1977
   (C) 1962   (D) jail

4. Fannie Lou was special because she—
   (A) dreamed every night   (B) fought for others
   (C) could vote   (D) grew food

5. The word "injustices" in line nine means—
   (A) things that are not fair   (B) jokes
   (C) acts   (D) fire alarms

Jacob Lawrence always knew he wanted to be an artist, and he worked very hard to learn to paint. Growing up in 1930 was not easy. Many people were out of work and poor. Young Lawrence walked miles each day from his home to the museums. He learned that museums did not tell much about black people. Jacob Lawrence decided he would tell their stories in pictures. He painted the story of Toussaint L'Ouverture, a slave who helped free the people of Haiti. He told the stories of Harriet Tubman and Frederick Douglass. Soon he became a *celebrated* artist. Today Lawrence's paintings hang in the same museums he walked long miles to visit when he was a child.

1. The best title is—
   (A) Art Museums
   (B) Jacob Lawrence
   (C) Living in 1930
   (D) Working Hard

2. Jacob grew up in—
   (A) a museum
   (B) Haiti
   (C) 1930
   (D) the South

3. Jacob visited museums to—
   (A) find work
   (B) stay warm
   (C) talk with friends
   (D) learn to paint

4. Jacob Lawrence—
   (A) still walks to museums
   (B) never became happy
   (C) became what he wanted
   (D) became a rich man

5. The word "celebrated" in line nine means—
   (A) famous
   (B) old
   (C) forgotten
   (D) busy

Many boys join a Boy Scout troop in grade school and drop out by high school. This was not the case for the "boys" from Troop 39. These *former* members of a Chicago Boy Scout troop met once a month for over 55 years.

For hundreds of boys, Troop 39 was a way to escape. Many came from a part of town where there was a lot of trouble. Their families did not have enough money. Pete Kukelski, the scoutmaster, made a difference in their lives. He often took the Scouts on camping trips. He taught them about nature and how to save lives. Most of all, he cared about them. Even after their leader died at age 75, the former Scouts still met at the home of his wife.

---

1. The best title is—
   (A) One Good Deed
   (B) Scouting Days
   (C) Boy Scouts for Life
   (D) Hard Times

2. The members of Troop 39 lived in—
   (A) Florida   (B) New York City
   (C) Chicago   (D) Cleveland

3. The Scouts met—
   (A) once a week   (B) once a year
   (C) once a month   (D) twice a year

4. You can tell that the Boy Scouts—
   (A) disliked Pete   (B) admired Pete
   (C) feared Pete   (D) alarmed Pete

5. The word "former" in line three means—
   (A) past   (B) younger
   (C) richer   (D) bad

Popcorn is one of the most popular snack foods of all time. In fact, popcorn is not a new snack food. Native Americans ate popcorn long before the Pilgrims arrived. They also made it into necklaces and used it to decorate their homes.

Popcorn pops because each little *kernel,* or seed, has water in it. When the kernel is heated, the water turns to steam and builds up until— pop!—it breaks out of the shell. Many people add something to their popcorn like butter and salt or melted cheese. Popcorn is one snack food of which millions of people say, "Too much is never enough."

1. The best title is—
    (A) Snack Foods
    (B) Native Americans Ate Popcorn
    (C) A Favorite Snack
    (D) Pilgrims

2. Today popcorn is—
    (A) full of sugar   (B) a new snack
    (C) not eaten   (D) a popular snack

3. Popcorn pops because—
    (A) it tastes good   (B) of steam
    (C) it grows slowly   (D) of the cold

4. From the story, you can tell that Native Americans—
    (A) did not like popcorn   (B) ate cold popcorn
    (C) used popcorn in many ways (D) ate only popcorn

5. The word "kernel" in line five means—
    (A) seed   (B) cup
    (C) leaf   (D) flower

Nearly everyone in the United States has eaten Girl Scout cookies. Few people know, however, that Girl Scout cookies have been sold since 1924.

Helen Smith was a Girl Scout leader in 1924. She thought that selling cookies would be a good way to *raise* money, so she went to a baker named Bob Wilson. He baked 35,000 cookies for the Girl Scouts. They sold them all in one week. Ten years later, they sold 114,000 boxes of cookies.

The Girl Scouts are still selling cookies to raise money. In 1994, they sold 166 million boxes of cookies.

---

1. The best title is—
    (A) Joining the Girl Scouts
    (B) A Lazy Baker
    (C) Selling Girl Scout Cookies
    (D) Learning to Cook

2. Bob Wilson was a—
    (A) Girl Scout   (B) truck driver
    (C) teacher   (D) baker

3. Every year Girl Scouts sell—
    (A) buttons   (B) pies
    (C) cookies   (D) flowers

4. The story suggests that Girl Scout cookies—
    (A) are not good   (B) are very popular
    (C) were not eaten   (D) were burned

5. The word "raise" in line five means—
    (A) make   (B) lose
    (C) cook   (D) dream

A class at Pearson School was learning that people should help each other. They said, "Let's find someone in our town who needs help." The class found an old woman who lived by herself. Her house needed many things done to make it look nice. The class decided to help.

First they *mended* a hole in the roof. Then they painted the whole house. They even planted new bushes in the front yard. After they finished, the woman had a nice-looking home.

It had taken five weeks of hard work, but the class was happy. They had worked to help someone.

1. The best title is—
   (A) A Class That Helped
   (B) Planting a Garden
   (C) Building a School
   (D) Finding a Lost Woman

2. To make the house look nice, the class—
   (A) broke the windows   (B) washed the dishes
   (C) painted it   (D) built a garage

3. The class worked for—
   (A) two days   (B) one month
   (C) three years   (D) five weeks

4. The story suggests that the class—
   (A) had many fights   (B) were poor workers
   (C) did not get paid   (D) did not like the woman

5. The word "mended" in line six means—
   (A) bought   (B) fixed
   (C) cleaned   (D) dug

When Margaret Patrick was about 75 years old and Ruth Eisenberg was 86, something unusual brought them together.

Margaret learned to play the piano when she was 8 years old. Ruth didn't learn to play until she was an adult. In 1982, both women got sick. Margaret lost the use of her right hand, and Ruth lost the use of her left hand. While they were *recuperating,* they met in a hospital. They were feeling sorry for themselves when a teacher suggested that they try playing the piano together. Margaret played the left hand and Ruth played the right. After a little work, the women were able to play together. They even gave concerts as "Ebony and Ivory."

---

1. The best title is—
   (A) Piano Music
   (B) Two Good Hands
   (C) Getting Sick
   (D) Music to Listen To

2. Margaret learned to play the piano—
   (A) at 75   (B) in 1982
   (C) as a child   (D) in a hospital

3. The two women were helped by—
   (A) a teacher   (B) Ruth's husband
   (C) other piano players (D) a doctor

4. Neither Margaret nor Ruth—
   (A) liked each other   (B) gave in to being sick
   (C) liked music   (D) minded getting sick

5. The word "recuperating" in line six means—
   (A) practicing   (B) growing up
   (C) painting   (D) getting well

In some parks, you play ball or watch animals wander about. In others, you swim or ride a bike or a roller coaster. Now there is a different kind of park—a butterfly park. In Pompano Beach, Florida, Butterfly World is a park that is also a farm. Imagine a huge screened "porch" that is larger than three football fields. Inside the porch is a forest of trees and plants from the hot, rainy parts of the world. Flying through this forest are more than 3,000 butterflies of 80 different kinds. It is an amazing sight to walk in this forest and see these butterflies at work feeding on *nectar* from flower blossoms.

---

1. The best title is—
    (A) Feeding Flowers
    (B) Parks
    (C) Butterfly World
    (D) Flower Farms

2. Butterfly World is in—
    (A) Florida   (B) a desert
    (C) New York   (D) a football field

3. Butterfly World is a—
    (A) football field   (B) roller coaster
    (C) front porch   (D) park that is a farm

4. Butterfly World was built so people could—
    (A) pick flowers   (B) count footballs
    (C) watch butterflies   (D) watch football

5. The word "nectar" in line nine means—
    (A) lost   (B) a sweet liquid
    (C) leaves   (D) rain

Can you pick up *The Guinness Book of Records* and not start reading it? Once you start, do you have trouble putting it down? Many people have the same problem. *The Guinness Book of Records* celebrated its 40th anniversary in 1995. At that time, it was the second-best-selling book ever.

Sir Hugh Beaver came up with the idea for *The Guinness Book of Records* in 1951. The first *edition* was sold in 1955 in England. The American edition was first sold in 1956. Since 1955, *The Guinness Book of Records* has been published in 37 languages, and by 1995 it had sold 77 million copies.

What's the oldest record in *The Guinness Book of Records?* St. Simeon the Younger spent the last 45 years of his life sitting on a stone pillar near Antioch, Syria. He died 2,000 years ago.

---

1. The best title is—
    (A) Sir Hugh Begins
    (B) The Oldest Record
    (C) A Best-Seller
    (D) Records Old and New

2. *The Guinness Book of Records* was sold first in
    (A) the United States   (B) England
    (C) Turkey   (D) Syria

3. *The Guinness Book of Records* has been printed in
    (A) 45 languages   (B) 77 languages
    (C) 2,000 languages   (D) 37 languages

4. You can tell that many people—
    (A) buy the book   (B) sit on pillars
    (C) read two languages   (D) dislike the book

5. The word "edition" in line seven means—
    (A) best-selling   (B) second
    (C) version   (D) silver

A. Exercising Your Skill

Read the story below. Note the underlined words. At the end is a list of numbered words. On your own paper, write a meaning for each word on the list. Use a dictionary if you need help.

Young Conrad Reed and his family relocated to North Carolina shortly after the conclusion of the American Revolution. One day in 1799, when Conrad was twelve years old, he escorted his younger brother and sister fishing in a nearby stream. No one caught any fish, but Conrad found a sizable nugget, or chunk of gold. Conrad presented the nugget to his father, who had an expert look at it. The man announced that the big nugget was not gold. The Reeds retained the nugget for three years anyway. At that time another expert contradicted the first one. The nugget, he said, was indeed gold. This time Conrad's father peddled it for $3.50. Too bad, for he later determined that the nugget was worth some $8000! When people heard about Conrad's discovery, they swarmed into the area looking for more gold. That was the onset of the first gold rush in the United States.

1. announced _____	7. peddled _____
2. conclusion _____	8. presented _____
3. contradicted _____	9. relocated _____
4. determined _____	10. retained _____
5. escorted _____	11. sizable _____
6. onset _____	12. swarmed _____

B. Expanding Your Skill

Compare your word list with your classmates' lists. Why did you write the meanings you did? Quite likely, you looked at the *context*—that is, the words and sentences around each underlined word. Looking at the context is a good way to figure out the meaning of a word you may not know. Choose five underlined words from Part A. Make up a sentence for each word you choose, and write it.

C. Exploring Language

Read the story below. Note the blanks where words should be. Think of a word to fill each blank. Complete the meaning of the sentence. On your own paper, write the number of each blank and the word that fills it.

Have you ever heard anyone use the (1)_____ "rich as Croesus"? Croesus [say "KREE sus"] was a king who (2)_____ many thousands of years ago. He was known for the gold that he owned. In fact, Croesus (3)_____ more gold than he could count! His wealth came from countries that he (4)_____ in wars. He also taxed any (5)_____ who came into his country. Over the years, many (6)_____ have been told about this (7)_____ king. One of these stories told how Croesus lost his (8)_____ . He made war on a great country, and lost his own (9)_____ in the end.

Compare your word list with your classmates' lists. Are the words the same? Are they different? Why?

D. Expressing Yourself

Choose one of these things.

1. Look up one of these old stories. Read it, then retell it to your classmates. Prepare well.

    Jason and the Golden Fleece
    The Golden Touch of Midas
    The Search for El Dorado

2. In a dictionary, look up the meanings of these words. Find out how they are all alike. Then write three other words that would fit with these words.

    alchemy   alloy   gild   gold leaf
        carat   lode   Forty-niner

3. Make a poster illustrating some of the many uses of gold.

Laura Jernegan wrote about how exciting life could be one hundred years ago. Young Laura and her little brother, Prescott, lived on a whaling ship with their parents. They sailed on the ship *Roman* for two years. The ship went through fierce storms and long weeks of calm when the winds never blew. Often they spent months without seeing land. Then, one month before they started home, some sailors on the *Roman* tried to steal the ship. A wild fight raged while Laura and her brother looked on in terror. Finally, Laura's father forced the bad sailors off his ship. Then he sailed it home with the nine sailors who had remained *loyal* to him.

1. The best title is—
   (A) An Exciting Storm at Sea
   (B) Children on a Whaling Ship
   (C) Traveling
   (D) The Fight at Sea

2. Laura sailed on the whaling ship—
   (A) with many friends   (B) all alone
   (C) for two months   (D) for two years

3. Laura's home for two years was *not*—
   (A) on the *Roman*   (B) with sailors
   (C) on an island   (D) with her family

4. Life on a whaling ship could be—
   (A) hungry   (B) dangerous
   (C) silly   (D) easy

5. The word "loyal" in line ten means—
   (A) weak   (B) true
   (C) false   (D) strong

Larry Luebbers liked the old ball park where his favorite team, the Cincinnati Reds, played their games. But it was going to be torn down for a new park. Larry was saddened by this. "I remember going to the park when I was a boy," he said. "When I heard they were tearing it down and selling parts of it, I wanted to buy a few chairs." Before he knew it, Larry had bought almost the whole park! He bought the fences and four hundred seats. He bought the scoreboard. He even bought a popcorn stand. Then he put them up in his own backyard. Now Larry is *contented*. He has a ball park just like the old one, but a bit smaller. Larry Luebbers, his friends say, is one of baseball's super fans.

---

1. The best title is—
   (A) The Cincinnati Reds
   (B) Baseball Parks
   (C) Backyard Ball Park
   (D) The Old and the New

2. Larry first went to the park to buy—
   (A) the fences   (B) the scoreboard
   (C) a few chairs   (D) a popcorn stand

3. Larry built a ball park—
   (A) in the old one   (B) in his own backyard
   (C) beside the new one (D) in another town

4. Larry would like—
   (A) to sell his park   (B) to enjoy his park
   (C) to paint chairs   (D) to buy more parks

5. The word "contented" in line nine means—
   (A) happy   (B) angry
   (C) lucky   (D) sad

One day Anna couldn't find her dog, Zorro. She had looked all around the yard. Then a little girl who lived next door said, "I know where Zorro is. He's up in a tree." Anna looked up and there in a tree was Zorro—wagging his tail. Anna called and Zorro climbed down.

The next day, Zorro climbed the tree again. He jumped to the lowest branch and then climbed *upward*. Every day after that, Zorro climbed the tree. Sometimes he even took a bone to chew.

Anna says, "My dog, Zorro, thinks he's a bird. He likes sitting in a tree."

---

1. The best title is—
   (A) A Dog and a Bird Become Friends
   (B) A Dog That Climbs Trees
   (C) A Dog That Can Fly
   (D) Finding a Lost Dog

2. Anna says that Zorro thinks he's a—
   (A) cat   (B) horse
   (C) rabbit   (D) bird

3. Sometimes when Zorro climbs a tree, he takes a—
   (A) friend   (B) pillow
   (C) bone   (D) bed

4. You can tell that Zorro—
   (A) has no teeth   (B) is afraid to climb
   (C) climbed the tree many (D) climbed the tree only once
        times

5. The word "upward" in line six means—
   (A) higher   (B) inside
   (C) under   (D) down

When Ralph Heard, Jr., of Atlanta, was just nine years old, he won the Junior Fire Marshal Gold Medal. This medal is the highest prize our nation gives to a young person for bravery at a fire.

One night while Ralph was asleep in his apartment, there was an explosion and a fire. Ralph was burned as he ran down the stairs to safety. Then he remembered his mother and younger sister. He ran back into the *inferno* and led them to safety. But Ralph wasn't finished. Once more, he ran into the flaming building. This time he knocked on the doors of the seven other apartments to warn the people inside. If Ralph had not acted so quickly, these people might have died.

---

1. The best title is—
   (A) Fire
   (B) Young Courage
   (C) Winning a Silver Medal
   (D) A Night in Atlanta

2. When Ralph won his medal, he was—
   (A) five years old   (B) seven years old
   (C) nine years old   (D) four years old

3. The Junior Fire Marshal Gold Medal is given to—
   (A) grown-ups   (B) young people
   (C) firefighters   (D) all of these people

4. Ralph showed that he was—
   (A) young   (B) afraid
   (C) brave   (D) quiet

5. The word "inferno" in line seven means—
   (A) door   (B) living room
   (C) roaring fire   (D) stairs

Linda was riding her bicycle home from the playground. As she neared her house, she saw a *crowd* of people. They were all looking up into a tree. Linda rode to the place where the people were standing. There, up in the tree, was Candy—her pet parrot.

While Linda was at the playground, Candy had flown out an open window. Other birds saw the parrot and began to attack it. Candy was sitting on a high branch, afraid to move. The people were shouting for Candy to come down. She wouldn't move. Then Linda called, "Here, Candy." The parrot flew into her arms. Linda took Candy into the house—and closed the open window.

1. The best title is—
   (A) A Visit to a Pet Store
   (B) A Broken Bicycle
   (C) Linda and Her Parrot
   (D) Feeding a Pet Bird

2. Linda rode home from the playground on—
   (A) a bus   (B) roller skates
   (C) her horse   (D) her bicycle

3. The people were shouting for Candy to—
   (A) fly away   (B) sing a song
   (C) come down   (D) stay in the tree

4. Linda closed the open window to—
   (A) keep out the snow   (B) make noise
   (C) keep Candy inside   (D) keep the house cool

5. The word "crowd" in line two means—
   (A) game   (B) group
   (C) room   (D) movie

It was Saturday morning, and Michael wanted to play with his friends. His mother told him that he had to work in the garden first. Michael was unhappy, but he took a shovel and started digging.

Michael had been digging for about an hour when he spotted something shiny in the dirt. Looking closely, he saw that he had *unearthed* a coin. He ran into the house and cleaned it. He was surprised when he found that it was a large one-cent piece. The coin was 188 years old. It turned out to be worth two hundred dollars. Michael was glad that his mother had asked him to work in the garden.

---

1. The best title is—
   (A) Michael and His Friends
   (B) Planting a Flower Garden
   (C) Playing on Saturday Morning
   (D) A Lucky Boy Finds a Coin

2. Michael was working —
   (A) at school
   (B) at the playground
   (C) in the house
   (D) in the garden

3. Michael found a—
   (A) one-cent piece
   (B) five-cent piece
   (C) dime
   (D) dollar

4. Michael was glad he worked in the garden because—
   (A) it was a sunny day
   (B) he was on vacation
   (C) he found the coin
   (D) he had no friends

5. The word "unearthed" in line six means—
   (A) spent
   (B) lost
   (C) dug up
   (D) given away

Just like many children, Libby liked to play with dolls. Rag dolls were her favorite. When Libby grew up, she still liked dolls. One year, she decided to make a rag doll. However, she wanted it to be different. She wanted to make a *gigantic* rag doll.

Libby used 1,300 feet of wool and four bedsheets. It took her one month to make the doll. When it was finished, it was 15 feet tall. At the time Libby made her doll, it was the biggest rag doll in the world.

Since Libby made her doll, Apryl Scott has made a bigger one. In 1990, Apryl made a rag doll that was 41 feet 11 inches tall. By now, someone else has probably made a bigger one.

---

1. The best title is—
   (A) The First Rag Doll in the World
   (B) Giant Rag Dolls
   (C) Children Like Dolls
   (D) Libby Grows Up

2. As a child, Libby liked to—
   (A) make her bed   (B) drive a car
   (C) play baseball   (D) play with dolls

3. To make the doll, Libby used—
   (A) four bedsheets   (B) two pillows
   (C) cotton sheets   (D) yarn

4. Making a doll this big must take—
   (A) many years   (B) many people
   (C) a million dollars   (D) a lot of work

5. The word "gigantic" in line four means—
   (A) paper   (B) tiny
   (C) huge   (D) live

When pets get sick, you can usually take them to an animal doctor or an animal hospital. Sometimes animals are so sick or hurt that you shouldn't move them. That's why Dr. Bird, a *veterinarian,* has a traveling hospital. Dr. Bird drives his hospital, which is really a van, to the animals.

Dr. Bird has run the hospital for over 10 years, and he has saved the lives of many pets. The van has an operating table, medicines, and everything else he needs to treat animals. Dr. Bird says that there will soon be many more traveling hospitals to help sick or injured animals.

1. The best title is—
   (A) Why People Get Sick
   (B) A Traveling Hospital
   (C) Dogs Make Good Pets
   (D) A Very Sick Animal

2. Dr. Bird has run the hospital for—
   (A) 12 years   (B) 10 years
   (C) 15 years   (D) 20 years

3. The story says that Dr. Bird's hospital has—
   (A) thick rugs   (B) no lights
   (C) toys   (D) medicines

4. Dr. Bird is—
   (A) a dentist   (B) an animal doctor
   (C) very young   (D) very sick

5. The word "veterinarian" in line three means—
   (A) animal doctor   (B) nurse
   (C) farmer   (D) truck driver

The Empire State Building is in New York City. It is a very tall building with many lights. Pat Watkins saw the Empire State Building when she visited New York. She fell in love with it. She even wrote a letter to the building saying how much she loved it and asking for a picture.

Two weeks later, Pat got a letter from the manager of the Empire State Building. He sent her a picture, a T-shirt, posters, and two books about the building. You can be sure that the next time Pat went to New York she visited her favorite *skyscraper*.

1. The best title is—
   (A) A Long Bus Ride
   (B) A Trip Across America
   (C) How to Draw a Picture
   (D) A Girl Who Loves a Building

2. The Empire State Building is—
   (A) in Florida   (B) very tall
   (C) falling down   (D) made of wood

3. The manager sent Pat—
   (A) a pen   (B) a map
   (C) two books   (D) two dollars

4. You can tell that Pat does *not*—
   (A) have a sister   (B) go to school
   (C) have a brother   (D) live in New York City

5. The word "skyscraper" in line nine means—
   (A) music store   (B) tall building
   (C) automobile   (D) movie

Like many young people, eleven-year-old Mel Fischer liked to read about sunken treasure. But not until he was a grown-up was Mel able to begin his search. In 1968, he went looking for the *Atocha*, a ship that had sunk hundreds of years before with *a fortune* in gold, silver, and jewels on board. Yet, Mel spent seventeen years looking for that ship. Along the way he ran out of money. Luckily, his helpers said they would work for nothing. Worse, his son and two other divers drowned. Then, in 1985, Mel saw his dreams come true. He found the *Atocha*. Mel is an old man now, but he has not stopped working. He runs a museum in Key West, Florida, where you can see many of the treasures he found on the *Atocha*.

---

1. The best title is—
   - (A) Treasure Hunter
   - (B) Pirate Treasure
   - (C) Reading About Adventure
   - (D) Key West, Florida

2. Mel Fischer became a treasure hunter when he was—
   - (A) eleven years old
   - (B) seventeen years old
   - (C) a grown-up
   - (D) nearly seventy

3. Mel found the *Atocha* in—
   - (A) 1948
   - (B) 1985
   - (C) 1968
   - (D) 1958

4. Searching for lost treasure is—
   - (A) not easy
   - (B) easy
   - (C) fun
   - (D) foolish

5. The words "a fortune" in line four mean—
   - (A) success
   - (B) fate
   - (C) luck
   - (D) riches

At the age of seventeen, Debbie is a first-class horse rider. She is also a top skier, tennis player, and swimmer. This may not sound so unusual. But Debbie is a special kind of sports lover. She was born with a *handicap*. Her right leg is only about half as long as her left leg. To correct this problem, she wears a heavy brace. This has never stopped Debbie, though. She has never used the words "I can't."

Like most riders, Debbie sometimes falls off. But she just gets up and tries again. "You can do anything you want to do if you put your mind to it," says Debbie.

1. The best title is—
   (A) Winning Rider
   (B) A Special Kind of Sports Lover
   (C) Problem Child
   (D) A Way with Horses

2. To correct her problem, Debbie—
   (A) uses her good leg
   (B) rides horses
   (C) wears a heavy brace
   (D) wins ribbons

3. When Debbie falls off, she—
   (A) asks for help
   (B) tries again
   (C) walks home
   (D) yells at her horse

4. Debbie's first love is—
   (A) skiing
   (B) tennis
   (C) swimming
   (D) riding

5. The word "handicap" in line four means—
   (A) problem
   (B) twin
   (C) secret
   (D) cold

The best rodeo cowboy who ever lived was a black man. A hundred years ago Bill Pickett grew up in Texas loving horses. It wasn't long before he went to work as a cowboy. Bill's job was to find steers that ran away. Like other cowboys, Bill used bulldogs. Then one day an angry steer ran off. This time, instead of calling his dogs, Bill jumped onto the animal's back. He quickly threw it to the ground and tied it with his rope. Soon Bill was catching all runaways this way. Not long after, Bill was doing it in rodeos. No matter how many others tried, no one could wrestle a steer as *skillfully* as Bill. Until he quit, Bill was the best. And the rodeo sport he invented, "bulldogging," is still as popular.

---

1. The best title is—
   - (A) The Only Black Cowboy
   - (B) The Man Who Invented Bulldogging
   - (C) Texas Cowboys and Bulldogs
   - (D) Rodeo Sports

2. Bill grew up in—
   - (A) rodeos
   - (B) Kansas
   - (C) Texas
   - (D) his uncle's home

3. Bill used bulldogs because—
   - (A) dogs liked steers
   - (B) other cowboys did
   - (C) runaways were dangerous
   - (D) steers liked dogs

4. From the story, you know that Bill—
   - (A) did not please his fans
   - (B) hated school
   - (C) rode a horse badly
   - (D) liked to ride

5. The word "skillfully" in line nine means—
   - (A) slowly
   - (B) easily
   - (C) stately
   - (D) friendly

Bob asked his mother what she wanted for her birthday. His eighty-year-old mother replied, "A ride in a balloon!"

Mrs. Stapleton, Bob's mother, always liked to do exciting things. When she was eighty years old, she wanted to float through the air in a balloon. Bob found a balloon to take his mother for a ride. It was a huge balloon with a basket hanging beneath. Mrs. Stapleton climbed into the basket with the pilot. They waved *farewell*, and up they went.

When they landed, Mrs. Stapleton said, "That was the best birthday present I've ever had."

1. The best title is—
   (A) Flying Kites
   (B) A Long Rest
   (C) A Bad Accident
   (D) A Ride in a Balloon

2. The story says that Mrs. Stapleton liked—
   (A) to sleep   (B) exciting things
   (C) her rocking chair (D) to stay home

3. In the story, Mrs. Stapleton was—
   (A) 40 years old   (B) 18 years old
   (C) 80 years old   (D) 70 years old

4. You can tell that Mrs. Stapleton—
   (A) cannot walk   (B) has two sons
   (C) was afraid   (D) liked her ride

5. The word "farewell" in line seven means—
   (A) sticks   (B) good-by
   (C) hello   (D) nothing

You know from science books that dinosaurs lived on earth millions of years ago. Do you have any idea why these huge *creatures* disappeared, though?

Some think that sickness killed all the dinosaurs. Others think that dinosaur eggs were eaten by other kinds of animals, and not enough baby dinosaurs were born. Still another idea is that something from outer space crashed into the earth. That would have caused great dust clouds. The sun would have been blocked for years, and the earth would have been too cold for dinosaurs. What is known is that about 60 million years ago, all the dinosaurs disappeared from the face of the earth.

1. The best title is—
   (A) Why Dinosaurs Disappeared
   (B) Dinosaurs and Other Animals
   (C) Terrible Sicknesses Killed the Dinosaurs
   (D) What Dinosaurs Did on Earth

2. Some think that other animals ate—
   (A) dinosaurs   (B) grass
   (C) plants   (D) dinosaur eggs

3. Great dust clouds might have blocked the—
   (A) rain   (B) moon
   (C) sun   (D) snow

4. From the story, you can tell that no one really knows—
   (A) why dinosaurs disappeared (B) when dinosaurs lived
   (C) what causes dust clouds   (D) how huge dinosaurs were

5. The word "creatures" in line three means—
   (A) spaceships   (B) living things
   (C) books   (D) objects

A. Exercising Your Skill

A good title will tell the main idea of a story in just a few words. Read the story below. Then write a title for it on your own paper.

(Title)
_____

Not all treasure hunters look for gold or jewels. Almost anything can become treasure. All it takes is for someone to want to collect something. For example, marbles that children play with are one kind of treasure. So are matchbook covers, fountain pens, postcards, dolls, old books, and sea shells. But these are only *some* of the things people collect. You may know that anyone can become a treasure hunter. All you have to do is start. From then on, it takes some money and some luck. But be warned. Once you start treasure hunting, you will never want to give it up!

On your own paper, write two sentences from the story that helped you think of your title.

B. Expanding Your Skill

Most stories or paragraphs have a sentence that gives the most important, or main, idea. It may not be the first sentence. It may be the last sentence, or it may be in the middle of the paragraph. Read this story to find the main idea sentence.

People of all ages collect coins. Some people collect coins from one country only. Other people collect coins from many countries, but all from the same years. There are people who collect coins because they are pretty. Others buy, trade, and sell coins. These people collect them to make money. Today coin collecting is a popular way to hunt for treasure.

On your own paper, write the main idea sentence.

C. Exploring Language

On your own paper, write a paragraph of four or five sentences. First choose one of the main idea sentences below. Then make notes about what you will write in your other sentences. These sentences should tell about the main idea. Next, write your paragraph. When you are finished, write a title that tells your main idea in two or three words.

1. Collecting things with another person is easier.
2. Adults and children can enjoy collecting.
3. Collecting matchbox cars is fun.
4. People who collect things must really like what they collect.
5. The best treasure hunters know a lot about what they collect.
6. Whole families can enjoy collecting.

D. Expressing Yourself

Choose one of these things.

1. Bring all or part of your collection to school. Give a talk to the class. Explain your collection.

2. Get together with any classmates who collect the same thing you do. Compare collections. Show your collections to your classmates. Be ready to answer their questions.

3. Some people collect large things like automobiles. Other people collect small things like marbles. Make a list of six different things people collect. Choose one thing from your list. Then write a sentence. Tell why you want to collect that thing.

4. Draw a poster that looks like a coin or a stamp. It may show a famous person or a famous place. Show your poster to your classmates.

Two walls in the dining room of the Phipps house are very unusual. They are covered with old pictures. The pictures are of members of the Phipps family who lived long ago.

Mrs. Phipps often tells interesting stories about the people in the pictures. One of them was given a medal for bravery in the Civil War. Another hid in a ship and took a *voyage* across the ocean when he was only eleven years old.

Mrs. Phipps is proud of her family of long ago. Maybe it would be fun to find out more about your family!

---

1. The best title is—
   (A) Ships That Cross the Ocean
   (B) Pictures of an Interesting Family
   (C) Living in an Old House
   (D) The Civil War

2. The pictures in the story are in a—
   (A) kitchen   (B) bedroom
   (C) garage   (D) dining room

3. One of the Phipps family won a medal for—
   (A) running   (B) bravery
   (C) spelling   (D) swimming

4. You can tell that most of the people in the pictures—
   (A) liked to swim   (B) are still alive
   (C) are not alive   (D) had brown hair

5. The word "voyage" in line six means—
   (A) picture   (B) trip
   (C) airplane   (D) fish

As the winter of 1988 grew near, people from many different countries came together to help free three gray whales that were trapped in the Alaska ice. If the whales were not freed, they would surely die. At first the people chopped away the ice, but it froze again. Then huge ships, called icebreakers, joined in the work. Helicopters flew in more people, food, and machines. After three weeks, a path was finally cut to the open sea. By then, one of the whales had died, but the other two were free. Now they could swim to Mexico, where they always spent the winter. For a *brief* time, at least, people of the world showed things could be done by working together.

1. The best title is—
    (A) Setting Whales Free
    (B) A Whale Hunt
    (C) Going to Mexico
    (D) An Alaskan Winter

2. The story takes place in—
    (A) Mexico   (B) Russia
    (C) Canada   (D) Alaska

3. The whales could not swim to Mexico because they were—
    (A) too tired   (B) afraid of the ice
    (C) too hungry   (D) trapped in the ice

4. When they were free, the whales swam to where it was—
    (A) dry   (B) windy
    (C) warm   (D) dark

5. The word "brief" in line nine means—
    (A) short   (B) long
    (C) cold   (D) scary

Mrs. Lake wanted to go to the drugstore. She put her huge dog, King, into the car and off they went. When they arrived at the drugstore, Mrs. Lake left the car running while she went shopping. King was left in the car.

Soon King moved into the driver's seat. His paw touched a handle and the car started to move. People on the sidewalk were amazed. It looked as if the dog were driving the car! The car went about one block before it *collided* with a parked car and stopped. Luckily, King was not hurt and the cars were not badly damaged.

1. The best title is—
   (A) Shopping Can Be Fun
   (B) Mrs. Lake Learns to Drive
   (C) A Dog Causes a Car Accident
   (D) A Dog Wins a Prize

2. Mrs. Lake went shopping at a—
   (A) drugstore　　　　　(B) library
   (C) farm　　　　　　　(D) school

3. In the story, King was—
   (A) given a prize　　　(B) left at home
   (C) killed　　　　　　(D) not hurt

4. People on the sidewalk were amazed because—
   (A) it was a nice day　(B) Mrs. Lake went shopping
   (C) dogs can't drive　(D) they saw a car

5. The word "collided" in line eight means—
   (A) washed　　　　　(B) crashed
   (C) flew　　　　　　(D) hopped

Diamonds are the most *valuable* stones on earth. One of the most famous stones is the Koh-i-noor—meaning "mountain of light," known for the bad luck it brings. This diamond was first owned by the rulers of India. When the Mongols, people from northern Asia, attacked India, the Mongol leader demanded all the jewels in the country—including the Koh-i-noor. But the Indian ruler said that the diamond would bring "bad luck and death to those who own it from this time forth." Since then, many different people have owned the diamond. Nearly every one of them died in some strange way. Now the Koh-i-noor is part of the crown that English kings and queens wear. To this day, no bad luck has come to them.

1. The best title is—
   (A) Diamonds
   (B) The King and Queen of England
   (C) The Bad-luck Diamond
   (D) Indian Jewels

2. The name "Koh-i-noor" means—
   (A) Great Diamond
   (B) bad luck
   (C) mountain of light
   (D) Indian Mongol

3. India was once attacked by—
   (A) bandits
   (B) diamonds
   (C) Koh-i-noors
   (D) Mongols

4. The leader of the Mongols was—
   (A) greedy
   (B) friendly
   (C) Indian
   (D) English

5. The word "valuable" in line one means—
   (A) old
   (B) costly
   (C) strange
   (D) ugly

Mrs. Lois Tinker bought a car for 1,638 snowballs!

It had been snowing for three days. A man who sells used cars had an idea. He said that he would give one dollar for every snowball anyone brought in—if the person bought a car. Lois and her family got busy. For four hours they made snowballs. They *packed* the snowballs into the trunk of their car and went to see the man. When they counted the snowballs, there were 1,638.

The man had a car for sale for $1,638. Mrs. Tinker gave the man the snowballs and took the car. It hadn't cost her any money.

1. The best title is—
   (A) A Terrible Snowstorm
   (B) How to Drive a Car
   (C) Buying a Car for Snowballs
   (D) A Trip to the City

2. For every snowball, the man paid—
   (A) ten cents   (B) one dollar
   (C) five dollars   (D) five cents

3. It had been snowing for—
   (A) two hours   (B) three days
   (C) four weeks   (D) five months

4. To get the car, Mrs. Tinker and her family—
   (A) sold apples   (B) went to the doctor
   (C) put on a show   (D) worked hard

5. The word "packed" in line five means—
   (A) lost   (B) put
   (C) opened   (D) ate

Different countries choose their leaders in different ways. But the most unusual way belongs to the League of Iroquois. Six nations, or tribes, of Native Americans (Indians) make up the League of Iroquois. They choose their leaders by the Great Law of Peace, which states that only Iroquois women can choose the leaders. The women must pick men, but if the leaders do not do a good job, the women are free to pick new ones. The Constitution of the United States was based partly on this Great Law of Peace. But the Constitution did not follow one important part. Women were not *permitted* to vote until 1920.

1. The best title is—
   (A) Native Americans
   (B) Voting for President
   (C) Choosing a Leader
   (D) The Constitution

2. The League of Iroquois has—
   (A) ten tribes   (B) women for leaders
   (C) men for leaders   (D) no women

3. The Great Law of Peace belongs to the—
   (A) English people   (B) League of Iroquois
   (C) United States   (D) Chinese people

4. The Iroquois nations—
   (A) do not like men   (B) wrote the laws
   (C) think highly of women (D) are afraid of women

5. The word "permitted" in line nine means—
   (A) refused   (B) stopped
   (C) voted   (D) allowed

Born in Texas in 1893, Bessie Coleman knew she wanted to do something exciting with her life. Then Coleman saw her first airplane, and she knew she wanted to fly. But no school would teach her because she was a woman, and a black woman at that. So Coleman went to Europe. At the age of twenty-eight, she became the world's first black woman to hold a pilot's license. Then she went home to fly in air shows. Soon she was called "Brave Bessie." Bessie Coleman had wanted to open a flying school for black women. Sadly, she never saw her dream come true. She was killed in a plane crash. But Coleman is still remembered today. A group of black fliers call themselves the "Bessie Coleman *Aviators*."

---

1. The best title is—
    (A) Learning to Fly
    (B) The First Black Woman Pilot
    (C) Air Show of Long Ago
    (D) How Women Learned to Fly

2. Bessie Coleman was born in—
    (A) Texas   (B) Oklahoma
    (C) Europe   (D) New York

3. Bessie Coleman learned how to fly in—
    (A) Texas   (B) Oklahoma
    (C) New York   (D) Europe

4. The best word to describe Bessie Coleman is—
    (A) careful   (B) daring
    (C) quiet   (D) Texan

5. The word "aviators" in line eleven means—
    (A) teachers   (B) doctors
    (C) fliers   (D) fighters

Moe Berg played baseball for the Brooklyn Dodgers and the Boston Red Sox. But he was not like other ballplayers. Moe Berg read up to twenty newspapers every day, and he spoke seven *foreign* languages. He was also a spy. After each baseball season was over, Moe went to a different foreign country. He took pictures and learned all he could. When he came home, he told the United States government what he had learned. The United States entered World War II in 1941. Just before the war began, Moe quit the Red Sox. He worked as a spy again during the war. After the war, Moe was told he had won many medals. He never took any, nor did he play baseball again. No one knows why.

---

1. The best title is—
   (A) World War II
   (B) Playing Baseball and Seeing the World
   (C) The Spy
   (D) The Ballplayer Who Was a Spy

2. Moe played for the Dodgers and the—
   (A) Giants   (B) Red Sox
   (C) Braves   (D) Astros

3. After each baseball season, Moe Berg—
   (A) rested   (B) learned a new game
   (C) played football   (D) went to another country

4. Moe—
   (A) liked medals   (B) liked secret codes
   (C) liked to read   (D) lived in fear

5. The word "foreign" in line three means—
   (A) hard to read   (B) from another land
   (C) out of date   (D) part of the United States

Think of the ways people cut down trees. They swing an axe or use a chainsaw to cut through the trunk until it *topples*. They might get a bulldozer and simply shove the trees over. These are not the ways big trees are felled, or knocked down, in the Solomon Islands of the Pacific Ocean, though. There the natives knock a tree down by yelling at it! That's right, yelling at it. Here's how they do it. Each morning, just before dawn, a group of natives creep up on a tree. Then, on signal, they scream at the tree at the top of their lungs. This goes on for thirty days. The Solomon Islanders believe that screaming at the tree kills its spirit. After the tree dies it falls over. According to the Islanders, their way always works.

1. The best title is—
   (A) Screaming and Yelling
   (B) Felling By Yelling
   (C) The Solomon Islands
   (D) Growing Trees

2. The Solomon Islands are in the—
   (A) Atlantic Ocean
   (B) Indian Ocean
   (C) Sea of Japan
   (D) Pacific Ocean

3. To fell a tree, Solomon Islanders take—
   (A) three days
   (B) two months
   (C) thirty days
   (D) thirty months

4. To the Solomon Islanders, trees are—
   (A) more than wood and leaves
   (B) strange plants
   (C) destroyed
   (D) always in the way

5. The word "topples" in line two means—
   (A) leans over
   (B) sways
   (C) dies
   (D) falls

There are many schools, but no school is like Bill Steed's in California. Bill's school is for frogs!

Every year there is a big contest for frogs. The frog that jumps the farthest wins. Many people send their frogs to Bill's school. He trains them to jump farther. The frogs do exercises to make them stronger. Bill plays music for the frogs and feeds them good food. He says, "A happy frog can jump better."

Bill doesn't promise that your frog will win first prize. But he does *guarantee* that every frog that comes to his school will be a better jumper.

---

1. The best title is—
   - (A) How to Catch Frogs
   - (B) A School for Frogs
   - (C) What Frogs Look Like
   - (D) Bill Finds a Lost Frog

2. Bill Steed's school is in—
   - (A) Mexico
   - (B) Florida
   - (C) California
   - (D) Texas

3. Bill trains frogs to—
   - (A) go to sleep
   - (B) jump farther
   - (C) read books
   - (D) write letters

4. Bill thinks that music makes frogs—
   - (A) weaker
   - (B) hungry
   - (C) dumber
   - (D) happier

5. The word "guarantee" in line nine means—
   - (A) promise
   - (B) drive
   - (C) sing
   - (D) look

Children in New York City always like to play at a playground. There are swings, slides, and sometimes toy horses. But the thing that some children liked to play with best was a real fire engine!

A teacher learned that the fire department had an old fire engine that it was going to get rid of. She went to the fire department and *inquired*, "Why not put the fire engine in the playground? The children would love to play on it." The fire fighters painted the engine bright red and put it in the playground. The children had fun making believe they were real fire fighters with their own fire engine.

---

1. The best title is—
   (A) A Terrible Fire
   (B) Toy Horses Are Fun to Ride
   (C) A Playground That Had a Fire Engine
   (D) A Woman Becomes a Fire Fighter

2. The fire engine at the playground was painted—
   (A) green   (B) yellow
   (C) red   (D) blue

3. The fire engine in the story was—
   (A) new   (B) old
   (C) on fire   (D) little

4. The story suggests that the fire department—
   (A) never puts out fires   (B) would rather paint
   (C) didn't need the fire   (D) doesn't like children
       engine

5. The word "inquired" in line six means—
   (A) forgot   (B) asked
   (C) drank   (D) slept

Roger Briles had a swimming pool in his backyard. The pool had a diving board. Roger couldn't believe what he saw when he looked at his pool one morning. There, on the diving board, was a car!

Roger ran to the diving board to look at the car. A man was inside. Roger asked, "How did you drive onto my diving board?" The man said that he had been driving for a long time and had become very tired. He had gone to sleep and the car had crossed Roger's lawn. It stopped on the diving board. He was lucky that the car hadn't *traveled* into the pool!

1. The best title is—
    (A) Cutting the Lawn
    (B) A Car on a Diving Board
    (C) A Trip Across the Country
    (D) Fun at the Beach

2. Roger's swimming pool was in his—
    (A) kitchen   (B) bedroom
    (C) backyard   (D) front yard

3. The man in the car had been—
    (A) playing baseball (B) fixing his car
    (C) cutting a lawn   (D) driving a long time

4. When the man became tired, he should have—
    (A) driven faster   (B) gone swimming
    (C) stopped and rested (D) run a race

5. The word "traveled" in line nine means—
    (A) cleaned   (B) gone
    (C) snowed   (D) jumped

A. Exercising Your Skill

In Unit 45 you read about Bessie Coleman. She was a daring person. The story does not say that Bessie was daring. But clues help you learn what Bessie was like:

1. No school would teach Bessie to fly.
2. Bessie went to Europe.
3. People called her "Brave Bessie."
4. Bessie Coleman died in a plane crash.

From these clues, you can guess what Bessie was like.

Read the story below. See what you can learn about Peggy.

Peggy looked off into the distance. She could hardly make out the shape of the car. Yet she knew it had to be Uncle Ted's car. It was five o'clock in the afternoon, and Uncle Ted always came home at that time. Peggy usually waited for him to drive up to the house before she ran out to greet him. Today, however, she was waiting by the gate. "This is my favorite time of day," she said to herself.

On your paper, write the answer that best tells how Peggy feels about her Uncle Ted.

1. Peggy is afraid of her uncle.
2. Peggy doesn't care about her uncle.
3. Peggy likes her uncle.

Now write two clues from the story that helped you choose your answer. Compare your answers with your classmates' answers. Did you write the same clues?

B. Expanding Your Skill

Work with a classmate. Write a new story about Peggy and her Uncle Ted. This time write clues to show that Peggy does *not* like her uncle. Remember, you do not want to *say* that she does not like him. You want readers to *guess* this from the words you use.

C. Exploring Language

When you read, you should not make wild guesses. A guess should come from clues in a story. For example, if you see your best friend run into school, you might guess that your friend has something important to do in school. But you cannot guess that your friend is happy about it. There are not enough clues for you to know that.

On your own paper, write what you can guess from these clues.

1. Four young people, all dressed up, are laughing happily as they walk down a street. They are carrying packages wrapped in brightly colored paper.
2. A woman comes out of a hospital. She is dressed in white. She is carrying a small black bag.
3. Lennie picked up his bat and glove. He walked to the door and opened it. Lennie saw that a heavy rain was falling.
4. Susan called out to Ellen. Ellen turned her head and walked away quickly.

D. Expressing Yourself

Choose one of these things.

1. Think of two scenes like the ones in Part C. Get together with three classmates and draw pictures of your scenes. Hold the pictures up before your classmates. See if they can guess what is happening in your drawings.

2. Listen to a movie or TV program with your eyes closed. The music can help you know what is happening. As you listen, see if you can tell when the story is happy, frightening, funny, dangerous, or mysterious. Choose a story from this book. Make a list of the kinds of music you would play when telling the story.